MEL ROBBINS

Turning Struggles into Strategies for Success

A Journey from Overwhelm
To Ownership

(*MEL ROBBINS LET THEM BOOK*)

BENJAMIN
SCARLETT

An *imprint* of THEORY, RESOLVER HOUSE (Pvt.) Ltd.

TITLE: *MEL ROBBINS TURNING STRUGGLES INTO STRATEGIES FOR SUCCESS*

Copyright © 2025 by *Benjamin Scarlett*

All rights reserved.

No part of this book may be reproduced, distributed, or transmitted in any form or by any means, including photocopying, recording, or other electronic or mechanical methods. Without the publisher's prior written permission, except for brief quotations embodied in critical reviews and specific noncommercial uses permitted by copyright law.

Publication: April 2025

ISBN: 978-1-967010-56-1 (Kindle Edition)
ISBN: 978-1-967010-55-4 (Paperback)

Contact Details:

+1 (689) 260-3550 (International)
+44 7951 726679 (United Kingdom Only)

Our Support:

Ukasharashidllc.com (Website)
info@ukasharashidllc.com (Email)

Publisher's Address:

30 N. Gould St., Ste R
Sheridan, WY 82801, USA

MANUFACTURED IN UNITED STATES OF AMERICA

Contents

INTRODUCTION 4

CHAPTER 01 11

CHAPTER 02 18

CHAPTER 03 25

CHAPTER 04 33

CHAPTER 05 40

CHAPTER 06 47

CHAPTER 07 55

CHAPTER 08 62

CONCLUSION 69

INTRODUCTION

The Quiet Struggle Behind the Spotlight

The world often meets brilliance when it's already polished, when the dust has settled, and the applause drowns out the silence that once consumed the soul behind the success. What it doesn't see—what it forgets or refuses to ask—is the raw, trembling journey that builds the scaffolding of a person's power. This is the invisible origin of Mel Robbins. A woman celebrated for her sharp mind, her command over crowds, and her groundbreaking ability to galvanize change within others, yet her roots are tangled in quiet, internal chaos few would dare imagine.

Long before her name graced bookshelves and echo chambers of influence, Mel lived in the margins of herself. She was not born with fire in her voices, she earned that roar, carved it from the silence of self-doubt and the aching hum of a life that didn't feel like hers. To understand her is to sit beside her—not just on stages or in media clips—but on the floor of her darkest moments, in the unspoken conversations with herself at dawn, in the gritty moments where survival was a whisper and not yet a battle cry.

She grew up in a world that, like most girls of her time, taught her to obey more than to question, to perform more than to be. Her mind was sharp, her instincts even sharper, but there was always an edge of unease, a sense that she was living a life she hadn't fully chosen. The rules were handed to her—get the grades, land the job, keep the smile in place. She followed them with the precision of someone terrified of failure but starving for something real. Her early years were an echo of effort and expectation, laced with the invisible burden of being "just fine" when she was, in fact, quietly fraying.

Law school wasn't so much a calling as it was a costume, something to wear that the world would applaud. And it did. On paper, Mel Robbins was thriving degrees, respect, a husband, children, a resume that made others nod with approval. But no applause could silence the sense of disconnection that grew louder each year. Like many high-functioning individuals, she wore her burnout well. She showed up. She delivered. And yet, beneath the surface, her life was slowly unraveling, stitched together by routines that no longer held meaning.

What makes Mel different is not that she fell apart. It's how she chose to rebuild—and what she discovered in the rubble.

There is something profoundly human in reaching the edge of your own life and realizing you don't recognize what's in front of you. That moment, for Mel, wasn't cinematic. It didn't come with lightning bolts or music swelling in the background. It came in the form of everyday dread—snooze buttons hit too many times, numbing routines, the fatigue of pretending. Anxiety began to take shape not as a passing emotion but as a full-time resident in her body. She wasn't living; she was reacting, barely managing, shrinking inside a life that seemed perfectly constructed to others but felt like a prison of her own making.

And yet, what looked like a breakdown would become her breakthrough.

There's a brutal elegance to the way Mel clawed her way out—not through grand gestures or miracle interventions, but through the smallest act of defiance: choosing to interrupt her thoughts. That's all it took. Not therapy at first, not medication, not motivational speeches. Just five seconds. A countdown. A simple, brilliant pause between impulse and action. It started with getting out of bed. And slowly, deliberately, it became a method of getting out of her own way.

This was not about willpower or discipline, not in the conventional sense. It was about returning to herself. About listening—not to the noise of self-criticism or societal programming—but to the quiet, insistent pull of intuition. She had ignored it for years. Now, it was time to trust it. That trust would become the cornerstone of her empire, and the very thing she would teach millions to rediscover for themselves.

Mel Robbins didn't build her name on theory. She built it on bruises and bad days, on vulnerability laid bare in front of audiences who were tired of perfection and hungry for truth. Her words resonate not because they are polished, but because they are lived. Because she dares to talk about marriage when it's messy, motherhood when it's unfiltered, and ambition when it collides with self-worth. Her life is not a highlight reel—it is a mirror. And the woman staring back dares others to look too, to see what needs changing, to stop waiting, to start moving, even when everything feels impossible.

Her journey defies genre. She is not a self-help guru, though she helps many. Not just a motivational speaker, though her voice fills rooms and lifts hearts. Mel is a translator between fear and action, a mapmaker for those lost inside their own hesitation. And perhaps most importantly, she is proof that transformation is not reserved for the chosen few—it is the birthright of anyone who decides to begin.

There's a reason her message resonates so deeply in this fractured, noisy world. People are tired. Tired of pretending. Tired of doubt. Tired of watching their lives from the sidelines. Mel stands as a lighthouse in that exhaustion, not because she promises to fix anyone, but because she shows what it looks like to fix yourself—not all at once, but one honest second at a time.

This isn't a fairy tale. It's a reclamation. It's the story of a woman who didn't reinvent herself so much as remembered who she was underneath the noise. Who took back her mornings, her body, her mind, her voice—and now invites the rest of us to do the same.

CHAPTER 01

Law, Limbo, and the Lie of Perfection

There is a certain seduction in the architecture of a perfect life—the way it gleams in photographs, sits neatly on resumes, and assures those around you that all is well. That seduction is as much a trap as it is a triumph, and for Mel Robbins, it was a stage built not for expression but for erasure. She built the life she thought she was supposed to want: Ivy League education, the law degree, the crisp suits and curated composure. But beneath the elegant exterior was a woman slowly vanishing inside the performance of success.

Mel didn't walk into the world of law because she loved it. She walked into it because it was solid, respectable, and impressive in all the ways that mattered to everyone but her. She was intelligent, ambitious, and could argue a point like fire moves through dry grass. But none of that necessarily meant fulfillment. It meant she could play the part. And for years, she did—exceptionally. She walked courtrooms with the kind of poise that commands respect, but even then, the gnawing ache of disconnection haunted her footsteps. There's something unspeakably lonely about being good at something that doesn't ignite your soul.

The legal world is no place for uncertainty. It rewards decisiveness, demands precision, and punishes any deviation from the mold. For a young woman trying to find herself, it was both a crucible and a coffin. Mel functioned like a machine—efficient, effective, admired—but at the cost of her own internal landscape. There were days she felt like a ghost in her own skin, going through the motions with a smile that didn't quite reach her eyes. The long hours, the polished conversations, the rigid expectations—they were suffocatingly familiar, like living inside a script someone else had written.

And yet, walking away didn't feel like an option. How do you abandon the version of yourself everyone else has accepted? The version that's paid off student loans, built a family, survived the gauntlet of adulthood with visible wins? The world does not always reward those who question the path. It applauds compliance, especially when it's wrapped in competence. So she stayed. She stayed long after her soul had started to leave the room. Because sometimes, it feels safer to be miserable in a known environment than to risk joy in the unknown.

Perfection is not a destination. It's a prison disguised as a penthouse, and Mel had reached the top floor. The view was stunning. The isolation was unbearable.

Marriage came with its own set of contradictions. She loved her husband. They were partners, parents, builders of a life. But love is not always a balm for spiritual dislocation. When you don't feel at home within yourself, even the most loving home can feel foreign. Their connection, while real, was strained by the silence Mel carried—an unspoken dissatisfaction that had no clear language yet. The pressures of parenting, work, and pretending created a brittle kind of intimacy. She didn't blame him. She didn't blame herself. But the quiet distance between who she was and who she was becoming widened each year.

Anxiety crept in like a fog. At first, it whispered. A little restlessness here, a little dread there. Then it roared. The smallest decisions became battles. Sleep was no longer rest—it was avoidance. Mornings became enemies. Tasks she once tackled with vigor now felt impossible. The cruel trick of anxiety is that it convinces you you're lazy, broken, weak—when in reality, you're burning energy just trying to exist. And because Mel looked "fine," no one questioned her unraveling. Not even her.

She became an expert at hiding. High-functioning, overachieving, master of disguise. Smiling in meetings while her heart raced. Hosting dinner parties while feeling like she might burst into tears. The disconnect was profound and exhausting. Somewhere along the way, she stopped seeing herself in the mirror. There was just a woman doing what needed to be done. A woman following rules she never wrote. A woman who wanted to scream but didn't know what words to use.

The lie of perfection is that it promises peace once you earn enough, achieve enough, impress enough. But perfection never delivers. It's a moving target. A mirage. And when you chase it long enough, it doesn't just disappoint—it devours. Mel was being devoured by her own ability to perform. The very skills that made her successful were the ones keeping her trapped. She knew how to keep going. She didn't know how to stop.

Rock bottom doesn't always look like a collapse. Sometimes, it looks like a woman silently losing herself while everyone else applauds. It looks like over-scheduling, over-drinking, over-thinking. It looks like waking up with a sense of dread you can't explain, and brushing your teeth anyway. It looks like being the friend who always has the right words, even when your own mind is chaos. Mel's descent wasn't public. It wasn't scandalous. It was ordinary and terrifying. And it was hers.

What she began to realize—slowly, painfully—was that something had to break. And that something was the illusion. She had built her life on a foundation of expectation, and the cracks were now too deep to ignore. The law, the image, the perfection—it had served its purpose. It had gotten her here. But it could not take her any further. If she wanted to live—not just exist—she would have to dismantle the architecture of her identity and start again.

And starting again didn't mean blowing up her life. It meant facing herself, fully and without judgment. It meant peeling back the layers of conditioning, of fear, of ego. It meant asking questions she didn't have answers to. Who am I, if I'm not the woman who always has it together? What do I want, beyond survival? How do I listen to myself when all I've heard for years is the noise of everyone else?

The shift began as a murmur. A journal entry. A tearful morning. A refusal to fake it one more day. She began to write again, to speak her truths in private before she dared share them publicly. She didn't know where it would lead. She only knew that silence was no longer an option. And so, she leaned into the discomfort. Into the mess. Into the possibility that maybe, just maybe, something better waited beyond the ruin.

There's something holy about a woman reclaiming her life—not in a dramatic, cinematic moment, but in the small decisions no one sees. Mel began choosing herself—not out of selfishness, but out of necessity. She chose stillness over productivity. Honesty over approval. And slowly, the world within her began to change.

This wasn't a reinvention. It was a resurrection. A return to the woman she had always been before the world told her who to be. She would find her voice again—not as a legal analyst, not as a perfect wife or model mother, but as Mel. Human. Flawed. Brave.

The law taught her how to argue, how to reason, how to defend. But it was life outside the courtroom that taught her how to feel. How to risk. How to live. And in the end, it wasn't the degrees or the accolades that saved her. It was the decision to stop pretending. To unlearn the lie of perfection. And to believe—against all odds—that she was allowed to begin again.

CHAPTER 02

The Five-Second Revolution

There are moments when the universe doesn't roar to get your attention—it whispers. The whisper comes at 6:00 a.m., when the alarm sounds and your hand hovers over the snooze button. It arrives in the blink between hesitation and action, the liminal space where old habits tug hard and new life waits patiently. For Mel Robbins, that whisper became a revolution—subtle, almost silly in its simplicity, and yet destined to change everything. It was not a grand philosophy or a carefully drafted blueprint. It was a countdown. Five seconds. A bridge between chaos and clarity. A practice so childlike in structure it was almost laughable. But that's where the miracle lay: in the profound simplicity of doing the thing before fear could talk you out of it.

The human mind is a storyteller, always narrating. Its favorite genre is fear. It warns, questions, speculates, and stalls. For Mel, those morning hours were a battleground. Not just of getting out of bed, but of getting back into life. After spiraling into the heaviness of anxiety, financial stress, and emotional fatigue, her brain had become a maze of excuses and hesitation. She had lived long enough on autopilot to know how swiftly minutes became hours, and how often the small act of starting became the mountain too steep to climb. Each morning she delayed, each minute she avoided doing what needed to be done, her life receded further into the fog of regret. And one day, staring at the television, watching a rocket launch into the sky, something broke open.

What if she launched herself out of bed like that rocket? What if she counted backward, not forward, like a launch sequence—5-4-3-2-1—and just moved before the excuses came? That impulse was ridiculous. Childish. But desperation is a curious sort of genius. It does not ask permission; it simply acts. And so, the next morning, she did it. She counted—five, four, three, two, one—and stood up. No hesitation. No second-guessing. Just motion.

That was the morning Mel Robbins discovered the key not just to her morning, but to her mind.

There is something deeply sacred about reclaiming agency in the smallest decisions. Society loves spectacle. We are trained to admire transformation when it is loud and luminous. But real transformation—lasting, gritty, defiant—often begins in silence. In the dark. In a cold bedroom before dawn. When Mel moved after that countdown, she didn't just get out of bed—she got back into her life. Her future would be built on those five seconds.

Behavioral science tells us what we instinctively know but often ignore: emotion kills momentum. Hesitation breeds fear. And fear masquerades as logic. "You're too tired." "It won't matter anyway." "Start tomorrow." Mel had lived those lies long enough. The five-second rule didn't give her more hours in the day—it gave her back her power. She began applying it to everything: returning difficult calls, sending emails, facing overdue bills, initiating hard conversations, even choosing to exercise. It worked because it interrupted the brain's default patterns. The countdown was a pattern-breaker, a cognitive intervention, a tiny act of rebellion against inertia.

And that's the thing about small acts—they add up. One honest conversation becomes two. One walk becomes a habit. One boundary makes space for ten. It wasn't about motivation anymore. It was about action. Five seconds was all it took to shut down the mental spiral and leap into life before fear had the chance to steal the wheel. Mel wasn't just surviving now; she was engineering a new internal infrastructure, one decision at a time.

To those watching from the outside, it seemed sudden. As if she had somehow flipped a switch and become a new woman overnight. But Mel knew better. The public often misunderstands private revolutions. They don't see the sweat behind the shift. They don't hear the quiet affirmations spoken into bathroom mirrors, the tiny negotiations made with one's own resistance. They see the TED Talk, the viral moment, the polished delivery. They don't see the mornings where she nearly cried from exhaustion before that countdown saved her again. Five. Four. Three. Two. One. Breathe. Move. Begin.

Mel was no longer trying to fix herself. She was no longer seeking salvation in someone else's strategy. She was living—imperfectly, boldly, honestly. And with each five-second act, her voice grew louder. Her confidence deepened. She started speaking about what she was experiencing, first with friends, then in interviews, then on stages. The idea spread like wildfire because it worked. It required no cost, no special equipment, no elaborate plan. It was accessible. Human. Achievable. And it brought people home to themselves.

There is a distinct kind of courage in declaring that the way we've been doing life isn't working, and then daring to do it differently. Mel was not preaching from a mountaintop—she was walking through the valley, inviting others to walk with her. Her message wasn't that she had all the answers. It was that you already have the answer—you just have to beat your brain to the punch. Her teachings became a mirror, reflecting the potential others had long buried beneath years of fear and failure.

The brilliance of the five-second rule was not in its novelty but in its accessibility. Anyone could do it. Everyone did do it. Students, soldiers, parents, executives—countless lives transformed not because they had the luxury of free time or resources, but because they chose to act instead of overthink. The stories came flooding in: marriages repaired, careers resurrected, addictions faced, dreams resurrected. All sparked by five seconds of courage. Five seconds that demanded nothing but a choice.

Mel understood then that transformation is never about massive, sweeping gestures. It's about micro-decisions. A thousand tiny choices that no one sees until they crystallize into a new life. The countdown was a tool, but the truth was even more powerful: your life comes down to the things you do, not the things you think. Thinking alone doesn't move you forward. Action does.

And the irony of it all? Mel hadn't intended to become a self-help leader. She wasn't trying to brand herself as a guru.

She was just trying to save herself. That's why her work resonated. Because it wasn't theoretical. It wasn't curated. It was born from lived chaos and reclaimed clarity. And it invited others to stop waiting for the perfect moment, the right time, the guaranteed outcome. It asked them to trust that action—small, fast, and brave—would always lead to more.

This was not a woman who had been handed confidence. She built it. She fought for it. She counted down into it, again and again. And even on days when the doubt came roaring back, she knew what to do. Five. Four. Three. Two. One. Move.

The five-second rule was never about being fearless. It was about being willing. Willing to act before fear became your master. Willing to begin, again and again, until your life started to reflect your intentions. It was about reclaiming time not just on the clock, but in the soul. Mel had discovered that the smallest window of decision could unlock the widest door of freedom. Not just once, but as a practice. As a lifestyle. As a devotion to living wide-awake.

She no longer waited for confidence. She created it. She didn't chase clarity. She moved toward it, five seconds at a time. And slowly, the life she once dreamed of—the one where she felt fully alive, deeply purposeful, radically present—was no longer a wish. It was her reality. Built not in leaps, but in choices. Lived not in theory, but in motion.

CHAPTER 03

Breaking the Loop of Self-Doubt

It begins in the quiet. Not in the thunder of catastrophe, not in the drama of ruin, but in the low, consistent hum of internal narratives that wear away at identity like water over stone. Self-doubt, so innocuous in its first whispers, takes up residence subtly—lurking behind ambition, masquerading as caution, wrapping itself around memory and future alike. For Mel Robbins, those loops of thought were not simply distractions; they were prisons without walls. They didn't scream, they echoed, constant and haunting. And like many who've lived beneath the weight of an overactive mind, she knew the cost of believing every fearful story it told.

Mel wasn't born into certainty. She was not raised to silence doubt with assurance. Her brilliance wasn't a birthright—it was a fight. A raw, undignified, deeply personal wrestle with the ghosts that clung to her spine: the feeling that she wasn't enough, the suspicion that failure would always catch up, the quiet ache of wondering if everyone else had figured out something she hadn't. And yet, amid those internal storms, she learned something sacred. Doubt, she realized, was not proof of inadequacy. It was simply the noise that rises when you dare to want more.

The mind, in its well-meaning dysfunction, craves safety. It clings to what is known, even when the known is misery. Self-doubt, then, becomes a warped form of protection. It says, "Don't try, because you might fail." It says, "Stay small, because the fall will hurt less." It wraps around the dreamer like a shroud and calls itself realism. But Mel began to see through it. Not all thoughts are truth. Not all inner monologues deserve an audience. And perhaps, she thought, the problem was not that she doubted herself—but that she believed the doubt so blindly.

There comes a moment in every life when the inner critic grows louder than any external voice. And for Mel, that moment came not in public, not under the spotlight, but in private reckonings. It came in front of mirrors. In silent car rides. In those fractured seconds before sleep when the brain replays every misstep like a broken record. And it was then that she decided to question the voice that had never been questioned before. Who was it that said she couldn't? Who assigned her these limits? Who taught her to shrink?

It was not a singular person, but a patchwork of experiences—rejections, comparisons, quiet shames—that had assembled the mask of doubt over time. But masks, no matter how familiar, can be removed. Mel began the unglamorous, deeply uncomfortable task of excavating her thoughts. Not to fix them. But to expose them. The loop of self-doubt thrives in secrecy. It festers in the shadows. Bring it into the light, however, and it weakens. The truth, once spoken—even if whispered—is a weapon.

She began replacing the questions that sabotaged her with questions that restored her. Instead of "What if I fail?" she asked, "What if I don't?" Instead of "Who am I to try?" she asked, "Who am I not to?" Instead of letting fear set the course, she allowed curiosity to take the wheel. She didn't need to become someone else. She simply needed to return to who she was before the world convinced her otherwise.

The turning point came not in a moment of success but in a moment of defiance. She looked at her doubt not as a prophecy but as a signal. If doubt showed up, it meant she was standing on sacred ground—stretching, reaching, daring. Doubt, it turned out, wasn't a stop sign. It was a signpost. Proof that something brave was underway. And so, rather than silence it, she reframed it. She invited it to walk beside her, but no longer allowed it to lead.

What Mel discovered through her own unraveling was that confidence is not the absence of doubt. It's the decision to move forward despite it. It is forged—not found—in the small daily acts of choosing courage over comfort. And those acts, done without applause, without audience, become the scaffolding of an unshakeable self. She built her voice like a cathedral, brick by stubborn brick, through moments of resistance and grace. She learned to interrupt her thoughts like she had once interrupted her inaction—with intention, with awareness, with five seconds of honest momentum.

The people who now looked to her for guidance often assumed she had overcome her doubts. But Mel never claimed to have conquered them. She had simply learned to manage them. To dance with them without surrendering to them. To listen without obeying. The human mind, after all, does not evolve out of fear—it evolves alongside it. And so, each time a doubt appeared, she welcomed it not as a failure, but as a sign she was growing.

Her mission expanded. She began teaching others what she had taught herself: that thoughts are suggestions, not orders. That confidence is built through evidence, not emotion. And that we are allowed to rewrite the scripts we've inherited. Mel helped thousands—millions, even—stand in front of their own mirrors and ask, "Who would I be without this doubt?" The answers that came weren't always clear. But the question itself was the doorway.

In the world she moved through—media, self-help, coaching—people often sought grand solutions. They wanted transformations to be loud, quick, permanent. But Mel knew better. True change whispers. It unfolds in the invisible victories: the email sent, the apology made, the dream revisited after years of neglect. Self-doubt loses power not through eradication but through irrelevance. The more you act in spite of it, the more it fades into background noise.

And so she lived accordingly. Not without fear. Not without faltering. But without surrender. Each speech, each book, each conversation was a testament to that quiet rebellion. She didn't wear armor; she wore truth. Her voice did not preach perfection—it offered permission. Permission to be messy. To begin anyway. To question what we're told about ourselves and author something truer.

What she modeled, more than anything, was humanity. She didn't float above the fray. She walked directly through it, offering her hand along the way. Her story was not one of sudden deliverance. It was the story of staying, showing up, choosing again and again to believe in something bigger than fear. It was about learning to trust herself after years of outsourcing that trust to others. And it was about helping others return to themselves in the same way.

There is a sacred kind of power in realizing you no longer have to live inside the thoughts that hurt you. That you can feel fear and still choose faith. That you can look doubt in the face and say, "Thank you for trying to protect me—but I'm safe now." Mel didn't kill her doubts. She made peace with them. And that peace made room for everything else: joy, creativity, connection, growth.

The loop of self-doubt—so ancient, so pervasive—is not unbreakable. It is simply habitual. And like all habits, it can be rewritten. It begins with a moment. A breath. A pause between fear and response. A voice, shaky at first, that says, "Maybe I'm not broken." A heart that whispers, "Maybe I'm ready." Mel heard that whisper once, in the ruins of her own self-belief. And instead of ignoring it, she listened. She followed it. She gave it volume.

That voice now echoes in the lives of those she's touched, not as an echo of her own, but as the rediscovery of theirs. Doubt may still visit. But it no longer stays. And where once there was a loop of fear, there now lives a loop of truth—a melody of courage, humming quietly, calling us home

CHAPTER 04

The Anatomy of a Moment

There are slivers of time that cleave reality before and after. These moments do not always announce themselves with fanfare. Sometimes, they arrive as quietly as a breath caught in the throat—insignificant in appearance, seismic in consequence. For Mel Robbins, one such moment lived in the space between chaos and choice. It was a morning like many others, heavy with dread, muffled by the inertia of a life unraveling in slow motion. Yet buried within that ordinariness, she found something extraordinary: the beginning of her return to herself.

The human spirit, though capable of immense resilience, often forgets its own strength. Life, with all its spinning pieces and compounded disappointments, can reduce even the brightest souls into dim versions of themselves. Mel knew that erosion intimately. It didn't happen overnight. The erosion crept in through exhaustion, through unspoken fears, through the accumulation of small compromises. She was not yet someone who the world turned to for guidance; she was someone simply trying to get out of bed.

There's a unique kind of despair that festers when the days blur into repetition and meaning seems elusive. She had dreams, yes—but they had begun to feel more like burdens than beacons. The distance between who she was and who she longed to be had grown into a chasm. She was watching her life unfold like a spectator, paralyzed by doubt, fogged by avoidance. But then came the moment—the moment that did not look heroic or bold but felt urgent in her bones.

It was a flash of instinct, a sudden awareness that if she didn't move—if she didn't act now—she might never act at all. Five seconds. That's all it was. The time between impulse and inhibition. The space where lives are either launched or left behind. She counted backwards from five and stood up, interrupting a pattern years in the making. It was absurdly simple. Almost laughable. But in that gesture, she found the first crack in her prison wall.

Mel would later come to name this act. She would teach it. Spread it. Change lives with it. But before the world recognized it as a tool, it was simply her salvation. The moment a woman, worn down by her own narrative, chose to write a new sentence. There is profound power in immediacy.

Procrastination may seduce the intellect, but it is presence that revives the soul. That moment—unremarkable to an outside eye—was the exact intersection where intention met action.

People often wait for the perfect time. The right circumstances. The ideal clarity. But Mel learned that clarity doesn't come before action; it comes because of it. Life, it seemed, wasn't going to deliver her from the darkness. She had to initiate the spark herself. And so she did—again and again. Five seconds to silence the critic. Five seconds to send the email. Five seconds to stand on a stage. Five seconds to press record. These micro-decisions became bricks in the architecture of a life remade.

Her story reminds us that transformation is not found in grand gestures. It is stitched together in the mundane, the repetitive, the seemingly unimportant acts of courage that most people never witness. The alarm goes off. The mind protests. And yet the body moves. That is where freedom lives—not in a changed world, but in a changed response to the world.

Mel came to understand the science behind her instinct. The brain, wired for protection, defaults to habit. Change threatens comfort. So when you hesitate, your mind intervenes—not to sabotage, but to safeguard. It whispers,

Wait. It warns, What if…? But by acting before that voice gains traction, by leveraging the raw momentum of instinct, you override the circuitry of fear. And the more you practice, the more you condition a new baseline for bravery.

What astonished Mel wasn't that it worked once. It was that it kept working. Repeated consistently, those five-second decisions formed a chain of defiance against stagnation. And with each action taken, her self-trust deepened. Confidence is not built by thinking—it is built by doing. You do not become brave by theorizing about bravery. You become brave by confronting the trembling, again and again, until the trembling transforms into readiness.

There is something almost rebellious about choosing yourself when the world has taught you to doubt. About taking that first bite of morning air when everything in your body pleads for escape. Mel became fluent in this rebellion. Not loud, not reckless—but steady, disciplined, devotional. She learned to trust her forward motion more than her fear. She stopped asking for permission. She stopped waiting for the right mood. She moved anyway.

As her own life shifted—first subtly, then monumentally—she began to recognize a truth long buried beneath motivational jargon: every life-altering decision begins with one tiny moment of interruption. A rerouting of autopilot. A refusal to obey inertia. The five-second rule, as it would later be known, was never about speed. It was about authority. Reclaiming the authority over one's own mind, one's own time, one's own story.

The world responded not just to the tool, but to the transparency. Mel never pretended to have it all figured out. She spoke from the trenches, not from the mountaintop. And so, people believed her. More importantly, they believed in themselves. Her message wasn't built on grandeur, but on relatability. If she could do it, from the floor of her despair, then maybe they could too. And they did—by the millions. Not because they had special talents, but because they chose to act while still scared.

The anatomy of a moment—the kind that alters trajectory—is composed of three things: awareness, urgency, and courage. Mel had them all. Not consistently, not perfectly, but enough to shift the ground beneath her feet. She became a student of those moments, documenting them, deconstructing them, helping others recognize their own. She taught people to listen to their inner knowing, not as a whisper of fantasy but as a compass. She offered them the framework to stop overthinking and start becoming.

There are few things more tragic than lives unlived due to hesitation. Dreams deferred because the moment to act was missed. Mel's gift to the world was not merely motivation—it was a method. A bridge between knowing and doing. She didn't ask people to feel ready; she taught them how to move before readiness. She didn't ask for belief upfront; she invited action as the birthplace of belief.

In truth, every person holds these moments inside them. Not just once in a lifetime, but countless times a day. Moments to speak, to ask, to leap, to let go. Most go unnoticed, suffocated beneath routine or silenced by fear. But when seen—truly seen—they can become portals. Mel Robbins chose to walk through hers. And in doing so, she lit the path for others.

Her story reminds us that time is not the healer. Action is. That the smallest step can fracture even the most rigid pattern. That five seconds can be the difference between another day lost and the start of a revolution—internal, intimate, sacred.

CHAPTER 05

The Unseen Engine of Reinvention

There is a kind of silence that follows a breakthrough—not the quiet of peace, but the stillness of recalibration. After the storm of transformation, when the adrenaline fades and the applause, whether internal or external, becomes a distant echo, there comes a moment when a soul sits with itself and begins to wonder: What now? For Mel Robbins, this stillness did not signal an ending. It announced the arrival of something deeper, something grittier. Reinvention. Not as a one-time event, but as a lifestyle—a relentless devotion to growth in the face of fear, fatigue, and familiarity.

Reinvention does not come dressed in gold robes or dramatic gestures. It often wears the plain clothes of discomfort. It tastes like vulnerability, stings like truth, and asks of you a surrender so thorough, you begin to question what parts of yourself are worth keeping. Mel did not embark on this process with a roadmap. She did not wake up with clarity or assurance. What she had was movement, and from that movement came evolution. She understood that the path to becoming is not paved in perfection but in radical self-honesty.

To reinvent oneself is to stand at the crossroads of who you've been and who you could become—and choose the latter without guarantees. Mel made this choice daily, privately, in ways that would never trend or trendset. She didn't just shift careers or aesthetics. She dismantled beliefs. She pulled back the layers of societal scripts and asked: What do I actually want? And more importantly: What am I willing to risk to get there?

Reinvention is not glamorous. It's lonely. It's frustrating. It's waking up to habits that no longer serve you and grieving the comfort they once gave. It's sitting with resistance and still choosing to write the email, start the workout, speak the truth. Mel came to recognize that most people are not afraid of change itself—they are afraid of the uncertainty it drags along. They are afraid of who they might lose, how they might fail, what ridicule might follow. And still, the ache of staying the same eventually outweighs the terror of becoming.

There's an undeniable magic in choosing your future over your past. That's what Mel did—not all at once, but layer by layer. She shed the idea that her worth was tied to productivity. She challenged the notion that fear was a stop sign rather than a signal. She rewrote her relationship with rejection, no longer seeing it as a verdict but as a redirection. These weren't grand proclamations. They were quiet rebellions, stitched into her routines, her responses, her resilience.

Her story is not about waiting for permission. It's about giving yourself the green light long before anyone else understands. When Mel stepped into the public eye—not just as a lawyer, or a talk show host, or a speaker—but as herself, unapologetically flawed and fully engaged, she began to build something extraordinary. Not a brand. Not a persona. But a mirror. One that reflected back to others their own hidden power.

People didn't flock to Mel because she had all the answers. They followed her because she asked the questions they were afraid to voice. She invited them into the mess of transformation, not the highlight reel. She admitted the panic behind her calm, the fear behind her fire. That transparency was its own revolution. In a world that rewarded polish and pretense, Mel dared to be real.

And realness, when embodied with courage, becomes contagious.

The journey of reinvention is littered with moments that test your sincerity. When the audience isn't clapping. When the bank account is low. When the doubt screams louder than the dream. Mel faced all of that. And rather than retreat, she leaned in. She used the discomfort not as a reason to stop but as evidence that she was stretching into unfamiliar territory—exactly where reinvention lives.

She taught others to do the same. Through her writing, her voice, her presence, she became a conduit for change. Not because she claimed expertise over life, but because she treated life as a continuous classroom. Every failure, every pause, every mistake—she mined them for insight. She modeled how to grow publicly, how to evolve visibly, without shame. And that made all the difference.

There is a great deal of courage required to outgrow your old self. To let go of stories you've told so long they've calcified. Mel Robbins became fluent in the language of letting go. Not of values or essence, but of limitations. Of narratives. Of roles that no longer fit. She didn't need a crisis to justify her shift. She allowed herself the grace to evolve simply because she desired more aliveness.

And reinvention, at its heart, is about aliveness.

It's about refusing to let your life shrink around your routines. It's about following the quiet nudges of curiosity, even when they lead into the unknown. Mel allowed herself to get curious again. To explore ideas without immediate payoff. To say yes to possibility and no to obligations that felt like slow poison. She tuned out the noise of "should" and reconnected to the pulse of her own desire.

This did not always please others. Reinvention, after all, disrupts expectations. When you begin to live more fully, you challenge the comfort of those still hiding. Mel learned to live with that discomfort. To accept that not everyone would understand, approve, or join her. She grieved those losses. But she never let them derail her.

What's more inspiring than the arc of her transformation is her refusal to make it a one-time event. She reinvents continually. As a mother, a speaker, a creator, a woman in her own becoming. Each phase of her life brings new questions, new challenges, new tools. And rather than cling to what worked before, she listens. Adjusts. Experiments. Evolves.

The world wants finish lines. Milestones. Definitions. But Mel offers something more liberating: permission to be a work-in-progress forever. To succeed and still want more. To grow and still question. To love your life and still change it. This philosophy has echoed through the millions she's reached. Not because it promises certainty, but because it celebrates agency.

To watch Mel Robbins, walk through her life is to witness someone reclaiming their narrative, moment by moment. Not because it's easy. But because it's true.

There is an engine beneath her reinvention that most never see. It's not just grit. It's not just timing. It's integrity. The willingness to live in alignment with her values, even when it costs her comfort. The commitment to keep showing up—not perfectly, but consistently. The humility to say, I don't know yet, but I'm willing to find out.

That is the spirit of reinvention. Not a finish line, but a rhythm. A pulse. A whisper that becomes a roar.

You can feel it in her words. You can see it in her work. You can sense it in her presence. And if you listen closely enough, you might recognize it in yourself.

Because reinvention is not reserved for the brave. It makes you brave.

Mel Robbins, by choosing herself again and again, has given countless others permission to do the same. And in that choosing, the world changes—not in giant leaps, but in the quiet revolutions of individual lives, waking up to their own possibility.

CHAPTER 06

The Bridge Between Doubt and Decision

There is a quiet tension that lives within all of us—an invisible tug-of-war between who we are and who we might become. It does not shout. It hums beneath the surface, in the moments we hesitate to raise our voice, to press send, to take the first step. Doubt is not a flaw in the system; it is the system warning us that change is coming. But what we do with that warning—that is where transformation begins. Mel Robbins knew this tension well. She did not run from it. She studied it, lived it, invited it to the table and asked it questions. She discovered that what many mistake for paralysis is often the threshold to courage.

In that brief, breath-held pause before decision, there lives a thousand stories: the voices of teachers who doubted us, parents who projected their fears, culture that insisted on smallness. These are the ghosts of hesitation. Mel, through her lived defiance and rigorous inner work, refused to let those voices dictate the rest of her life. She made a practice of interrupting the narrative, re-authoring the script in real-time. Where others paused and retreated, she leaned in. She came to understand that the brain, when confronted with change, will default to safety. But safety, unchecked, becomes a prison.

What separates those who remain stuck from those who leap is not talent, intelligence, or privilege. It is the ability to act in the face of uncertainty. To close the gap between doubt and decision. Mel's revolutionary insight—that hesitation is the enemy of momentum—became a guiding principle for millions, not because it was a novel concept, but because it was delivered with the fierce intimacy of someone who had stood in that exact place. Someone who had stared at the ceiling at 3:00 a.m. and whispered, I can't live like this anymore.

It was there, in that private darkness, that the bridge was built. Five seconds. A window. A countdown. Not to perfection, but to motion. Mel's 5 Second Rule was not about strategy; it was about biology. About understanding the speed with which our fear sabotages our intentions, and how easily that sabotage can be stopped with a simple, physical, decisive act. It was elegant in its simplicity and profound in its impact.

It empowered people to reclaim the moment—the holy, irreversible now—before doubt could hijack it.

Decision-making, as Mel uncovered, is not about certainty. It is about ownership. There is no such thing as a perfect decision. There is only the decision you are willing to stand behind, build upon, learn from. This reframe liberated countless people from the tyranny of overthinking. It freed them from the myth that clarity must precede action. Mel taught that clarity follows action. That doing is how we learn who we are, not thinking.

She did not arrive at these truths from an ivory tower. They were carved out of panic attacks, job loss, marital struggles, and a decade of surviving on fumes. They were forged in the real heat of real life. When Mel speaks of decision-making, it is not theoretical. It is cellular. She made a decision every time she got out of bed while depression clawed at her. She made a decision every time she showed up on a stage, trembling. She made a decision every time she chose to be vulnerable in a world that rewards façades.

Each of these moments was a stitch in the fabric of her authority—not the authority of dominance, but of embodiment. People trust Mel not because she claims perfection, but because she dares to be seen in process. In her most human, she becomes most powerful. And power, she reminds us, does not always roar. Sometimes it's the whisper that says, go anyway.

The space between doubt and decision is also where self-trust is born. Not the glossy confidence sold in commercials, but the kind that develops when you keep promises to yourself. Mel did not become trusted by others until she learned to trust herself. That trust came from small acts of courage repeated daily. Not grand gestures, but consistent ones. Writing the page. Saying the truth. Leaving the thing that no longer fit. Starting again.

These decisions often looked irrational to outsiders. That's the nature of bold moves—they are misunderstood by those who have not yet given themselves permission to leap. Mel walked away from careers, projects, and roles that no longer resonated with her evolving values. She did not apologize for her pivots. She honored them as signs of growth. She reminded the world that reinvention is not betrayal—it is an act of self-loyalty.

Still, decision-making does not guarantee smoothness. It simply guarantees movement. Mel never promised an easy path. What she offered instead was a map through the fog. A way to act with integrity even when the outcome is uncertain.

She gave voice to the intuition we've all silenced, and she modeled how to listen to it again. The decision, she showed, is not the end. It is the beginning of the next becoming.

Her own life continued to unfold as a testament to this. As her platform grew, so did the stakes. More eyes. More criticism. More pressure to conform to the image the world expected. But Mel refused to harden into a caricature of herself. She continued to make decisions that preserved her freedom. Sometimes that meant saying no to lucrative offers. Sometimes it meant pulling back from visibility to restore her soul. These were not decisions made from fear, but from alignment.

This, too, was a radical teaching: that saying no is also a decision. That not now can be as powerful as yes. That boundaries are a form of self-respect. Mel dismantled the myth that success means perpetual acceleration. She reminded us that the most potent decisions are not always forward—they are inward.

And so, the bridge between doubt and decision remains a sacred place. It is the site of every meaningful change. Every apology. Every risk. Every love letter. Every reinvention. Mel Robbins stood on that bridge, again and again, and decided to cross. Not because it was easy, but because it was necessary.

To decide is to say: I am the author now. That is the essence of her message—not just motivational fluff or surface-level encouragement—but a deep, resonant call to personal sovereignty. Mel believed in the power of one small act to redirect a life. She witnessed it in her own. She witnessed it in the countless people who used her work as a springboard into their own revolutions.

This is the paradox of decision: it is both the smallest unit of agency and the greatest act of power. When you decide, you collapse the infinite and step into the actual. You stop living hypothetically and begin living specifically. You take responsibility—not just for the result, but for the process. For the journey. For the self you are willing to become along the way.

And that is the heartbeat of Mel Robbins' legacy—not a catalog of achievements, but a constellation of moments where people, inspired by her truth, chose differently. Chose bravely. Chose themselves.

CHAPTER 07

The Power of Choosing Yourself

Choosing yourself—such a simple phrase, yet one that holds the deepest weight in a world that consistently asks for sacrifice, for conformity, for the comfort of fitting in. To choose yourself is not a rebellious act in the traditional sense. It does not seek to tear down what is. Instead, it seeks to nurture what could be, to give rise to a new possibility within you that has always longed for the light but has been too hidden beneath the layers of external expectations and self-doubt.

The journey of choosing yourself is not a path that always feels glamorous. It's not adorned with the glitz and glamour of the life you see portrayed in magazines or on social media. It doesn't come with an immediate applause or approval from the world. No, choosing yourself is a quiet, yet deeply powerful act. It requires you to stand in the face of uncertainty, to dare to walk away from the comfort of what you know, and to stand firm in what you are becoming, even when it isn't clear what that will look like.

Mel Robbins, in her own life, exemplified this journey. When she first embarked on her path of self-empowerment, she didn't start with a blueprint. She didn't have the perfect strategy or even a clear understanding of the magnitude of what she was about to undertake. All she had was a quiet, persistent desire to reclaim her life from the haze of self-doubt, from the exhaustion of trying to be everything to everyone except the most important person: herself.

Her story, like so many others, begins with a profound realization: to make the kind of impact you wish to have on others, you must first choose to believe in your own worth. Mel had to untangle herself from a web of insecurities, fears, and external definitions of success. She realized that much of the dissatisfaction she had with her life stemmed from trying to live up to ideals that weren't even hers. She was living according to the terms of others—their expectations, their demands, their values—and in doing so, she had neglected to ask herself one simple question: What do I truly want?

This is where the journey begins for so many. The realization that, at some point, we must stop looking to the outside for validation and instead turn inward. Choosing yourself is not about becoming self-centered or narcissistic. It is about giving yourself permission to live for your own approval, to be the author of your story, and to trust that your voice matters.

When Mel began to choose herself, she wasn't just choosing her career or her success—she was choosing her peace. She was choosing the quiet moments, the inner stillness that could only be found when she no longer felt compelled to meet the demands of a world that constantly pulled her in a hundred directions. It was in those moments of solitude, of looking inward, that Mel found the courage to take the steps she needed to change her life.

Choosing yourself means recognizing that your worth is not dependent on the applause or approval of others. It means letting go of the societal script that says you must constantly hustle, strive, and prove yourself in order to be seen. It means rejecting the false narrative that your value is contingent upon your productivity or your ability to fit into predefined roles. In choosing yourself, you give yourself permission to be fully, unapologetically you.

For Mel, this wasn't a one-time decision. Choosing yourself is not a momentary act. It is a continuous, daily practice. It is waking up each morning and deciding that today, you will honor your own needs, your own desires, your own boundaries. It is about saying no to things that drain you, saying yes to what nourishes you, and finding the courage to step into the unknown—even when the path ahead seems foggy.

But there is power in the fog. There is strength in the uncertainty. And in that space, Mel found herself, not in a grand epiphany but in the small, consistent choices she made every single day to honor who she was becoming, not just who she had been.

In choosing yourself, you learn to recognize that there is no one else who can live your life for you. There is no one else who can walk in your shoes, who can feel your emotions, who can hear your thoughts as you do. The most powerful thing you can do is to align yourself with your truth, to trust that your unique perspective has value, and to believe that your presence on this earth matters.

As Mel made the decision to choose herself, she discovered something revolutionary. She learned that when you prioritize your own well-being, when you stop sacrificing your happiness for the comfort of others, you not only transform your own life—but you become a beacon of light for those around you. Choosing yourself doesn't just free you;

it frees others. It inspires them to look inward and ask the same question: What do I need to do in order to honor myself?

Through her own personal transformation, Mel's message became clear: Choosing yourself is the key to unlocking the life you desire. It is the gateway to personal freedom, to peace, to fulfillment. It's the moment you stop living for anyone else's approval and start living for the truth that resides deep within you.

Choosing yourself is a radical act in a world that tells you to give, to please, to perform. But it is in this act of self-affirmation that you find your true strength. It is in this act that you step into your full potential. And it is in this act that you begin to craft a life that is uniquely yours, a life filled with purpose, meaning, and the profound satisfaction of knowing that you have chosen to live it on your own terms.

The beauty of choosing yourself is that it isn't a destination. It's a journey. And each step forward is a testament to the strength, courage, and resilience that resides within you. So, just as Mel did, you too can begin today. You can choose yourself, one small decision at a time. You can say, Yes, I am worthy of this life. Yes, I am worthy of my dreams. Yes, I choose to honor who I am becoming.

In that choice, everything changes.

CHAPTER 08

Embracing the Imperfections of Growth

In the vast, ever-expanding landscape of personal development, there lies an unspoken truth that, though often hidden beneath layers of self-judgment and societal pressure, quietly asserts itself as the most important realization in any transformational journey: growth is imperfect. It is messy, it is awkward, it is far from linear, and it demands patience from those who wish to embrace it. Yet, it is within the imperfections of growth that we find the deepest wisdom and strength.

There is something profoundly humbling about this truth. We live in a world that glorifies perfection, a world where flawless images, smooth achievements, and polished successes are held up as the ultimate standard. The idea that growth should be seamless, effortless, and always forward-moving is a narrative that is often ingrained in us from a young age. We are taught to measure our success in terms of the visible, the concrete, the finished product. Yet, for those who have ventured into the realm of self-improvement, there comes a point when it becomes abundantly clear: the true beauty of personal transformation is found not in the flawless end result, but in the raw, unrefined process that precedes it.

Mel Robbins, in her own evolution, discovered this truth on her journey. At the outset of her personal growth, she was not the poised, self-assured figure that many would come to know her as. She was a woman standing on the precipice of change, unsure of what lay ahead, yet determined to forge her own path. But like all those who venture into the world of self-discovery, Mel quickly learned that transformation is rarely a smooth, uninterrupted ascent. It is full of detours, missteps, and setbacks—each one offering an opportunity to learn, to grow, and to emerge stronger than before.

The idea of embracing imperfection is not one that comes naturally to many. We are, after all, conditioned to seek out the perfect, the pristine, and the ideal. It's easy to look at someone who has achieved success and think, They've got it all together. But behind every success story is a tangled web of failures, doubts, and challenges—each moment contributing to the unique, often untold story of how someone reached the point of success they now occupy.

Mel Robbins' path to becoming a widely respected thought leader and motivational speaker was filled with such moments. There were periods of doubt, times when she wondered if she was truly capable of the life she envisioned for herself. She faced failures—some large, some small—that could have easily derailed her journey. But instead of letting these moments define her, Mel chose to embrace them as integral parts of her growth. She began to understand that perfection was not the goal. The goal was progress, the ability to keep moving forward despite the imperfections, the missteps, and the roadblocks that inevitably appeared along the way.

It was through this mindset shift that Mel truly began to thrive. She stopped viewing her mistakes as evidence of failure and instead saw them as necessary stepping stones. In fact, she learned that it was in her imperfections—the moments when she felt least confident, least capable—that she discovered her greatest strength. These imperfections were the fertile ground from which her resilience grew, the very qualities that allowed her to rise again and again, even when the path seemed unclear.

And so, as Mel's message evolved, it became clear that embracing imperfection was not just a personal truth—it was a universal one. Growth is not about striving for an unattainable ideal. It is about embracing the full spectrum of human experience, with all its messiness, unpredictability, and rawness. True growth is about surrendering to the process, about recognizing that perfection is a construct, and that the beauty of life lies in its imperfection.

For many, this realization is freeing. It releases them from the oppressive grip of comparison, of self-doubt, and of the unrealistic expectations that they have placed upon themselves. It encourages them to stop looking for the perfect moment, the perfect solution, or the perfect version of themselves. Instead, it teaches them to embrace the imperfect journey, to celebrate the small wins along the way, and to trust that the progress they are making—no matter how small—is leading them exactly where they need to go.

There is immense power in this shift. To let go of the need for perfection is to release yourself from the exhausting cycle of trying to meet external standards. It is to recognize that the only measure of success that truly matters is the one you set for yourself. And it is to understand that every imperfect step you take, every moment of doubt, every failure, and every triumph contributes to the person you are becoming. Growth is not about erasing your flaws or hiding your mistakes. It is about learning to embrace them, to learn from them, and to use them as fuel for your continued evolution.

For those who are brave enough to embark on the journey of personal transformation, embracing imperfection becomes a foundational principle. It is the recognition that you are not broken, that you do not need to be fixed. You are whole, even in your most imperfect moments. And it is this wholeness, this acceptance of who you are right now, that allows you to continue growing, to continue evolving, and to continue pursuing the life you desire.

Mel Robbins became a living testament to this truth. She built her success not on a foundation of perfection, but on a foundation of resilience, authenticity, and an unwavering belief in the power of personal growth. She was willing to be imperfect, to be human, to stumble and fall, and to keep going despite it all. In doing so, she became not just a voice of encouragement for others, but a living example of the power of embracing the full spectrum of life—the beautiful, the messy, and everything in between.

So, as you embark on your own journey of growth, remember this: perfection is not the goal. The goal is progress.

The goal is to continue moving forward, to continue learning, and to continue evolving into the best version of yourself. And in that process, allow yourself the grace to be imperfect. Allow yourself the room to stumble, to fail, and to rise again. For it is in the imperfections that you will find your greatest strength, and it is through this acceptance of imperfection that you will unlock your true potential.

The road ahead will not always be easy. There will be days when you feel like giving up, when you wonder if the progress you're making is enough. But remember that the journey itself is the reward. Each step you take, each lesson you learn, and each imperfection you embrace brings you closer to the person you are meant to be. So, let go of the need for perfection. Embrace the messiness of growth. Trust in the process, and know that every imperfect moment is leading you to the life you are destined to create.

CONCLUSION

The Power of Becoming

In the quiet spaces between moments, when the world slows down just enough to catch its breath, there is a deep truth that resonates within us all—a truth that transcends the noise of everyday life, the endless demands of modern existence, and the weight of self-doubt that so often clouds our vision. It is the truth that our journey of becoming is, at its core, a sacred one. It is a path that is both uniquely our own and yet deeply connected to the collective experiences of humanity. And in this journey, we come to understand that true success is not measured by the accolades we collect, nor by the external markers of achievement. True success lies in the quiet confidence of knowing ourselves, in the quiet revolution that occurs within when we choose to embrace our full potential, imperfections and all.

The journey we embark upon is one that never truly ends, for becoming is not a destination but an ongoing process. It is the constant evolution of who we are, the shedding of layers we have outgrown, and the embracing of the new versions of ourselves that emerge as we dare to grow. And in this ever-unfolding transformation, there is beauty. The beauty lies not in the destination, but in the journey itself. In the small moments of courage, the fleeting sparks of inspiration, and the quiet triumphs that no one else may see but which resonate deeply within us. These moments, these experiences, are the true markers of progress, for they reflect the inner shift—the shift from self-doubt to self-belief, from fear to courage, from stagnation to growth.

It is easy to become consumed by the noise of the world—the constant push to achieve more, to be more, to measure up to impossible standards that never seem to waver. But the true measure of a life well-lived is found not in external validation, but in the deep sense of fulfillment that arises when we align with our true selves. It is the quiet, powerful realization that we are enough, just as we are, and that we are deserving of every opportunity, every challenge, and every moment of growth that comes our way. It is the peace that comes when we stop comparing our path to others, and instead, trust that our unique journey is unfolding exactly as it should.

As we reflect on the lives of those who have inspired us, whether through their words, their actions, or their presence, it becomes clear that their true greatness lies not in their perfection, but in their willingness to embrace imperfection. They have dared to be vulnerable, to show up as their authentic selves, to stumble and fall and rise again. And in doing so, they have created a ripple effect—a wave of inspiration that encourages us all to do the same. To trust in the process. To trust in our own worth. To trust in the power of becoming.

And so, as we stand at the crossroads of our own personal journeys, it is important to remember that the only true measure of success is not the accumulation of accolades, but the quiet satisfaction that comes from living authentically, from choosing to become who we are meant to be, one courageous step at a time. It is the understanding that growth is not a linear path, but a winding road full of twists, turns, and unexpected detours. And it is in these moments of uncertainty, when the path ahead is unclear, that we often find the greatest growth.

To become is to release the need for perfection and to embrace the process of unfolding. It is to understand that we are not defined by our mistakes, but by how we rise from them. It is to trust that every challenge we face, every obstacle we encounter, is not a roadblock, but an opportunity to learn, to evolve, and to become stronger. In the face of adversity, we have the power to choose our response. We can allow ourselves to be defeated by the circumstances, or we can choose to rise—stronger, wiser, and more determined than ever before.

Mel Robbins, through her own personal transformation, has shown us that becoming is not about having it all figured out, but about having the courage to keep moving forward despite the uncertainty. She has shown us that greatness is not measured by the absence of failure, but by the willingness to continue, to persist, and to embrace the messiness of life. She has taught us that it is not about waiting for the perfect moment to take action, but about taking action right now, with all our imperfections, with all our doubts, and with all our fears. For it is in these moments of imperfect action that we find our true power.

As we move forward in our own journeys, let us remember that the process of becoming is not something to be rushed. It is not something to be measured against the timelines or expectations of others. It is a deeply personal journey, one that unfolds in its own time, at its own pace. And so, we must be gentle with ourselves. We must trust that each step, no matter how small, is part of the larger story of who we are becoming. There is no finish line, no ultimate goal that will mark the end of our journey. There is only the continual process of unfolding, of becoming, of evolving into the person we are meant to be.

In the end, the most important thing we can do is to honor ourselves. To honor the quiet courage it takes to show up every day, to do the work, and to continue moving forward, no matter the obstacles. To honor the wisdom that comes from the experiences we have lived, and to trust that every step we take brings us closer to the person we are meant to become. We may never fully understand the vastness of our own potential, but we can take comfort in knowing that we are on the path, and that with each passing day, we are becoming more fully ourselves.

And so, we leave behind the need for perfection, the constant striving for an unattainable ideal, and embrace the truth that becoming is the journey itself. The growth, the challenges, the victories, and the failures—they are all part of the grand story of our lives. And in this, we find peace. We find purpose. We find the power of becoming.

MEL ROBBINS

Turning Struggles into Strategies for Success

A Journey from Overwhelm
To Ownership

(*MEL ROBBINS LET THEM BOOK*)

BENJAMIN
SCARLETT

Printed in Great Britain
by Amazon